Number Resources YEAR 5
For Numeracy Lessons
by Annie Owen

Contents

Introduction

The elements of numeracy – whether knowledge, understanding or skills – follow a loose hierarchy. The structure is sometimes obvious, as in the need to understand fractions and decimals before looking at equivalence. However, in other areas the sequence can be blurred. Which comes first, knowing squares of numbers to 10×10 or being able to find the factors of any number to 100? Being able to order a set of decimals, or being able to round them to the nearest integer?

Children can learn such concepts at different times and in different orders. All teachers know that it is nigh impossible to predict how much will be absorbed by any individual child at first meeting and that concepts need to be revisited after a suitable gap. Because children themselves choose what is absorbed and what is rejected any collection of children is naturally a mixed ability group.

Given these two factors – the need to revisit concepts and the need to cater for a wide range of ability – schools need resources for numeracy which are flexible and easily adaptable. This book is an attempt to provide just that.

Many of the resources are easily changed to provide experience at different levels. There is also a good deal of cross-referencing, several resources being of use for a particular concept.

The Teacher's Notes are organised around statements from the National Numeracy Framework (NNF). They are not comprehensive, being a support resource, but may provide teachers with ideas for areas of the number curriculum not covered here. The division of the ideas into books for separate years is for ease of access, but the resources can be used across all ages as ability requires. The additional resource book, *Teacher's Templates for Numeracy KS2,* gives further flexibility for revisiting concepts at different levels of difficulty and hence also supports mixed ability teaching.

Vocabulary

All vocabulary used on the worksheets is consistent with the recommendations of the NNF Mathematical Vocabulary Book.

A note about order

For ease of use, the concepts are met here in the order of the NNF's Teaching Programme. This is not necessarily the order in which they are taught, this being loosely defined by the Framework but finally decided by each school.

A note about problem-solving

Wherever possible, the activities have been opened up to allow children exploration. Theoretically, therefore, very many activities can be mapped to :

NNF: 79 Solve mathematical problems or puzzles; recognise and explain patterns and relationships, generalise and predict. Suggest extensions asking 'What if …?'

However, this would be repetitious and this mapping is hence only made where it is the main objective of the activity.

A note about calculators

Although some guidance is given about the use of calculators – by including a calculator icon on the worksheets which might need one – their use is at the discretion of the teacher. A pupil who is particularly adept at, for example, vertical written calculations, might be asked to attempt some activities without the calculator. For other children, some of the worksheets without the icon may be a little too difficult for them and a calculator would enable them to produce the number patterns, etc. necessary for drawing conclusions about the behaviour of numbers. This can also aid pupil confidence, as such children will be more willing to take part in plenary discussions if they are 'sure' that their working is correct.

Teacher's notes

NNF: National Numeracy Framework

TTN KS2: Teacher's Templates for Numeracy KS2 *(published by Evans)*

NNF mappings in bold type are Key Objectives for this year group.

1 Earthquake!

NNF: 3	Read and write whole numbers in figures and words, and know what each digit represents.
9	Order a set of integers less than 1 million.
11,13	Round any integer up to 10000 to the nearest 10, 100 or 1000.

The children should find that there is no simple relationship between the number of deaths and the size of the earthquake. It would be interesting in a plenary to discuss what are the factors which make some earthquakes more dangerous (high population, poor building construction, ease of rescue, forewarnedness, etc.)

Discuss also which is the most useful 'rounding', e.g. do we need to know deaths to the nearest 10? Does rounding a 5-digit number to the nearest 10000 (Iran 1978) give aid agencies enough information? etc.

Other real-life statistics useful for this area of the NNF are: lengths of rivers, height of mountains, populations, etc.

2 The odd calculator and Reverse challenge

NNF: 3	Read and write whole numbers in figures and words, and know what each digit represents.
45, 47	Use known number facts and place value for mental addition and subtraction.

'The odd calculator' also reinforces the importance of zero as a place-holder.

Children having difficulty can model the numbers using the Multibase pictures in TTN KS2 and the Place-value holder in this book (Worksheet 3).

3 Place value holders

NNF: 3	Read and write whole numbers in figures and words, and know what each digit represents.
7	**Multiply and divide any positive integer up to 10000 by10 or 100 and understand the effect**
29	**Use decimal notation for tenths and hundredths.** Know what each digit represents in a number with up to two decimal places.

As the same pieces of equipment (eg the thousand cube) are used here to stand for very different things, it is better if the two halves are not introduced together.

Either enlarge the holders, or reduce the Multibase cards (TTN KS2) so that they fit each other. You may also want to make a larger one to take Multibase equipment. Model numbers, and the multiplication and division of 10 and 100. Children can hence see, for example, individual sticks of 10 (longs) being swapped for 100s (flats) and can see or feel the divisions on the apparatus. When they are happy with the concept, switch to the cards and eventually to digits only.

4 Max and min

NNF: 15	Calculate a temperature rise or fall across 0° C.

Use this worksheet as an introduction to counting across the zero point.

Other areas which offer scope for this concept are: height and depth above and below sea-level, debits and credits at the bank, time-lines with the child's birth as zero.

5 My own rules

NNF: 17	Recognise and extend number sequences formed by counting from any number in steps of constant size, extending beyond zero when counting back.
79	Recognise and explain patterns and relationships.

This worksheet is self-explanatory.

6 Is it true?

NNF: 19   Make general statements about odd or even numbers, including the outcome of sums and differences.

       81   Make and investigate a general statement about familiar numbers or shapes by finding examples that satisfy it.

Proving something isn't true at this level is easy – all we have to do is find one example which doesn't fit and the statement is obviously wrong. Proving something IS true, however, is difficult. At the primary level, it is only necessary to find some examples which agree with the statement, although this isn't really a sufficient proof. The worksheet, therefore, requires either one example which disproves or a handful of statements which agree with the statement.

Sometimes, facts can be explained using diagrams:

'Two odd numbers add up to make an even number' is always true because:

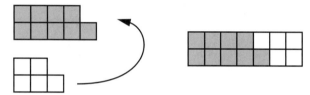

This is a better proof and you might wish to ask more able pupils to try to prove some of the other statements this way as an extension.

7 Abacus multiples

NNF: 19   Recognise multiples of 6, 7, 8, 9, up to the 10th multiple.

       59   **Know by heart all multiplication facts up to 10 × 10.**

This worksheet begins with multiples of 3 and 4, to make sure the children understand the concept while working with numbers they know well. They should continue for multiples of 6, 7, 8 and 9. Multiples which can be made are:

Of 3:   3, 12, 21, 30, 102, 111, 120, 201, 210, 300
Of 4:   12, 120, 300
Of 5:   30, 120, 210, 300
Of 6:   12, 30, 102, 120, 210, 300
Of 7:   21, 210
Of 8:   120
Of 9:   None

As an extension, ask the children to change the number of beads or the number of prongs. For the latter, they could use calculators if the numbers are getting too large.

8 Disco lights

NNF: 17   Recognise and extend number sequences formed by counting from any number in steps of constant size

       19   Recognise multiples of more than one number. For example, multiples of both 2 and 3 (see NNF examples page 19)

This is a good activity for introducing the concept of common multiples. Red and blue will flash together on every multiple of 12, blue and green on every multiple of 20, red and green on every multiple of 15, and all three on every multiple of 60. So, they all flash together every minute, and so will flash together 60 times in the next hour.

9 Square patterns

NNF: 21   Know squares of numbers to at least 10 × 10.

The shapes combine to make a square thus:

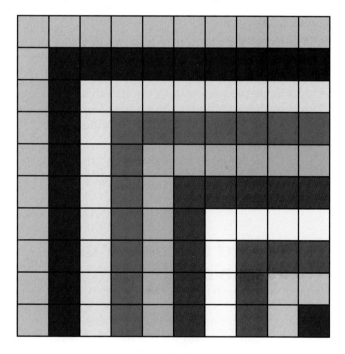

Help the children , if necessary, to see that the number of cubes which make each 'L' shape are the same numbers as seen in the growing number pattern (i.e. an 'L' shape will always be an odd number, and the next-door shapes are hence consecutive odd numbers).

Can they also see that the square numbers on the multiplication square are at the corners of squares? You could ask the children to draw round the squares on a board or OHP.

10 Factor pairs

NNF: 21 Find all the pairs of factors of any number up to 100.

At the plenary, tease out how the factor pairs can be seen in the list of factors, eg:

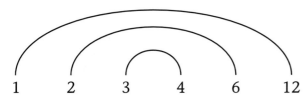

11 Equivalent fractions

NNF: 23 Recognise when two simple fractions are equivalent

You may wish to use the large multiplication square (TTN KS2), cut into strips so that the children can lay them side by side. If the children have not met the concept before, you will need to explain how equivalent fractions can be made through multiplication:

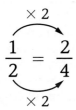 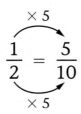

12 Farey lattices

NNF: 23 Use fraction notation and the vocabulary numerator and denominator.

23 Order a set of fractions

These graphs are named after a mathematician – Farey – who devised them. Children should find that equivalent fractions all lie on the same straight line. If they draw a line of fractions equal to a half, then fractions smaller than a half will lie below this line and those greater than a half will lie above it. The bottom two graphs are for experimentation.

13 Domino fractions

NNF: 23 Order sets of fractions such as 2, $2\frac{3}{4}$, $1\frac{3}{4}$, $2\frac{1}{2}$, $1\frac{1}{2}$, and position them on a number line.

The children should notice that the dominoes (TTN KS2) and their rotations fall roughly symmetrically about 1. That is, if the fraction is very close to 1 on the left, then its inverse will be very close on the other side. The whole line will look like this:

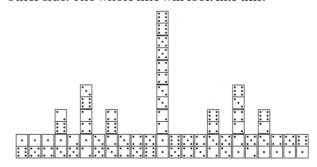

14 Connect 4

NNF: 25 **Relate fractions to division,** and use division to find simple fractions of numbers

This is a game for 2–4 children. The bottom section needs enlarging and cutting up to make cards, which are shuffled and placed face down. The children all work on the same grid, each with a different coloured pen. They take turns to take a card, work out the answer and decide which number to circle on the grid. The first to get 4 in a line (diagonally also counts) is the winner.

15 Decimal shades

NNF: 29 **Use decimal notation for tenths and hundredths.**
Know what each digit represents in a number with up to two decimal places. Order a set of numbers or measurements with the same number of decimal places.

39 Derive quickly or continue to derive quickly all two-digit pairs that total 100 (e.g. 43 + 57)

These grids can also be cut up and pasted onto the 'greater than' strip on worksheet 18. Make sure at the plenary that all understand that the two parts add up to make 1.00.

16 Decimal jigsaw

NNF: 29 **Use decimal notation for tenths and hundredths.**
Know what each digit represents in a number with up to two decimal places. Order a set of numbers or measurements with the same number of decimal places.

This worksheet is self-explanatory. It focuses the mind on to which decimal place changes as the numbers grow. Children can make their own using the Decimal Grid in TTN KS2.

17 Target

NNF: 29   Order a set of numbers or measurements with the same number of decimal places.

This worksheet is self-explanatory.

18 Percentage shades

NNF: 33   Begin to understand percentage as the number of parts in every 100

These grids can also be cut up and pasted onto a number line, as in worksheet 15. A large wall-line would make an attractive display.

19 Garden planner

NNF: 31   **Relate fractions to their decimal representations**

33   Begin to understand percentage as the number of parts in every 100

At the plenary, make sure that the children's figures add up to make 100%, 1.00, 1. More able children could be asked to give the fractions in lower terms (eg $\frac{1}{5}$).

20 Money dominoes

NNF: 31   Recognise that, for example, 0.07 is equivalent to $\frac{7}{100}$; 6.35 is equivalent to $6\frac{35}{100}$; particularly in the context of money *(see NNF examples page 31)*

This activity links coins, money notation and percentages. There is not an explicit reference to this in the NNF, but it is a fundamental concept and is implied in many places.

The dominoes could be combined with the Fraction/Decimal dominoes in TTN KS2 for a more difficult version.

21 Work it out! and Think of a number

NNF: 43   Develop further the relationship between addition and subtraction.

53, 55   Understand the effect of and relationships between the four operations

75   Choose and use appropriate number operations to solve problems, and appropriate ways of calculating: mental, mental with jottings, written methods, calculator.

If some of the children find two-stage calculations difficult, begin with some one-stage examples.

The 'Think of a Number' (THOAN) activity is an excellent 5-minute filler once the children have got used to the format. Let the children use whatever jottings, calculators, etc. they need. The main aim here is understanding the inverse operations, rather than the calculations.

22 Arranging digits

NNF: 49, 51   Use informal pencil and paper methods to support, record or explain additions and subtractions. **Extend written methods to: column addition/subtraction of two integers less than 10000**

This will be too tedious if the children are not proficient at this method of addition and subtraction. In such cases, let them look for solutions with a calculator.

At the plenary, see if the children can find any rules which would help them always get the largest/smallest for any arrangement.

23 Brackets

NNF: 53, 55   Begin to use brackets.

71   Develop calculator skills and use a calculator effectively.

Most calculators now have algebraic (does × and ÷ first) logic. There should be a lot of different examples generated for a good plenary discussion.

24 Seven sentence strings

NNF: 61   Use doubling or halving, starting from known facts. For example:

double/halve any two-digit number by doubling/halving the tens first;
double one number and halve the other;
to multiply by 25, multiply by 100 then divide by 4;
find the x16 table facts by doubling the x8 table;
find sixths by halving thirds.

61   Use factors (e.g. $8 \times 12 = 8 \times 4 \times 3$).
63   Use closely related facts (e.g. multiply by 19 or 21 by multiplying by 20 and adjusting; develop the $\times 12$ table from the $\times 10$ and $\times 2$ tables).
63   Partition (e.g. $47 \times 6 = (40 \times 6) + (7 \times 6)$).
63   Use the relationship between multiplication and division.
65   Use known facts and place value to multiply and divide mentally.

Most of these concepts have been met before, and therefore we provide here a consolidation activity. Asking for the 'longest possible strings' stops children making trivial statements and also provides some fun at the plenary.

25 Grid gaps

NNF: 67, 69 **Extend written methods to: short multiplication of HTU or U.t by U; long multiplication of TU by TU**

This worksheet should not be attempted unless these are methods the children have already met. Ask the children to write the full sum under each problem. For example, under the first problem write: $6 \times 173 = 1038$. Emphasise the answers in the plenary.

26 Palindromes

NNF: 79 Solve mathematical problems or puzzles, generalise and predict.
71   Develop calculator skills and use a calculator effectively.

The additions and subtractions will always produce palindromes, the latter having to be the same length. Some small palindromes have squares which are palindromes (eg $22 \times 22 = 484$).

27 How long/how far?

NNF: 82–89 **Use all four operations to solve simple word problems involving**

numbers and quantities based on 'real life'
Explain methods and reasoning.
71   Develop calculator skills and use a calculator effectively.

Although the answers to these can be amusing, the main aim is the development of the strategies. It is very important to therefore discuss the children's methods at every opportunity.

28 Perimeters and areas

NNF: 79 Solve mathematical problems or puzzles, recognise and explain patterns and relationships, generalise and predict.
Suggest extensions by asking 'What if...?'
82–89 **Use all four operations to solve simple word problems involving numbers and quantities** based on measures

The closer a rectangle can get to a square (for a set perimeter), the larger the area. The longer and thinner the rectangle (for a set area), the greater the perimeter.

29 The grand tour

NNF: 82–89 **Use all four operations to solve word problems involving numbers in 'real life', money** ...including making simple conversions of pounds to foreign currency.

Let the children plan the holiday excursion themselves, perhaps going to other countries, or in a different order. Currency converters can be found on the WWW, and some 'tourist' rates appear in the daily papers. What about a group of British students going to the Far East? or Africa?

Mapping to the National Numeracy Framework – Year 5

		1	2	3	4	5	6	7	8
3	Read and write whole numbers in figures and words, and know what each digit represents	●	●	●					
7	Multiply and divide any positive integer up to 10000 by 10 or 100 and understand the effect			●					
9	Order a set of integers less than 1 million	●							
11, 13	Round any integer up to 10000 to the nearest 10, 100 or 1000	●							
15	Calculate a temperature rise or fall across 0° C				●				
17	Recognise and extend number sequences formed by counting from any number in steps of constant size, extending beyond zero when counting back					●			●
19	Make general statements about odd or even numbers, including the outcome of sums and differences						●		
19	Recognise multiples of 6, 7, 8, 9, up to the 10th multiple							●	●
21	Know squares of numbers to at least 10 x 10								
21	Find all the pairs of factors of any number up to 100								
23	Recognise when two simple fractions are equivalent								
23	Use fraction notation and the vocabulary numerator and denominator								
23	Order a set of fractions								
23	Order sets of fractions such as $2, 2\frac{3}{4}, 1\frac{3}{4}, 2\frac{1}{2}, 1\frac{1}{2}$, and position them on a number line								
25	Relate fractions to division, and use division to find simple fractions of numbers								
29	Use decimal notation for tenths and hundredths. Know what each digit represents in a number with up to two decimal places			●					
29	Order a set of numbers or measurements with the same number of decimal places								
31	Relate fractions to their decimal representations								
33	Begin to understand percentage as the number of parts in every 100								

9	10	11	12	13	14	15	16	17	18	19	20	21	22	23	24	25	26	27	28	29
●																				
	●																			
		●																		
			●																	
			●																	
				●																
					●															
						●	●													
						●	●	●												
										●	●									
									●	●										

9

Mapping to the National Numeracy Framework – Year 5 *Continued*	1	2	3	4	5	6	7	8
39 Derive quickly or continue to derive quickly all two-digit pairs that total 100 (e.g. 43 + 57)								
43 Develop further the relationship between addition and subtraction								
45, 47 Use known number facts and place value for mental addition and subtraction		●						
49, 51 Use informal pencil and paper methods to support, record or explain additions and subtractions. Extend written methods to: column addition/subtraction of two integers less than 10000								
53, 55 Understand the effect of and relationships between the four operations								
59 Know by heart all multiplication facts up to 10 x 10							●	
61 Use doubling or halving, starting from known facts. For example: double/halve any two-digit number by doubling/halving the tens first; double one number and halve the other; to multiply by 25, multiply by 100 then divide by 4; find the x16 table facts by doubling the x8 table; find sixths by halving thirds								
61 Use factors (e.g. 8 x 12 = 8 x 4 x 3).								
63 Use closely related facts (e.g. multiply by 19 or 21 by multiplying by 20 and adjusting; develop the x12 table from the x10 and x2 tables).								
63 Partition (e.g. 47 x 6 = (40 x 6) + (7 x 6)).								
63 Use the relationship between multiplication and division.								
65 Use known facts and place value to multiply and divide mentally								
67, 69 Extend written methods to: short multiplication of HTU or U.t by U; long multiplication of TU by TU								
71 Develop calculator skills and use a calculator effectively								
75 Choose and use appropriate number operations to solve problems, and appropriate ways of calculating: mental, mental with jottings, written methods, calculator								
79 Recognise and explain patterns and relationships					●			
79 Solve mathematical problems or puzzles, generalise and predict								
81 Make and investigate a general statement about familiar numbers or shapes by finding examples that satisfy it						●		
82–89 Use all four operations to solve simple word problems involving numbers and quantities based on 'real life'								
82–89 Use all four operations to solve simple word problems involving numbers and quantities based on measures								
82–89 Use all four operations to solve word problems involving numbers in 'real life', money ...including making simple conversions of pounds to foreign currency								
82–89 Explain methods and reasoning								

9	10	11	12	13	14	15	16	17	18	19	20	21	22	23	24	25	26	27	28	29
						●														
												●								
													●							
												●		●						
															●					
																●				
														●			●	●		
												●								
																			●	
																	●		●	
																		●		
																			●	
																				●
																		●		

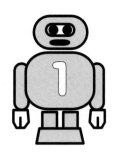

Earthquake!

Below is a table showing how many people were killed in some of the major earthquakes this century.

Year	Place	Magnitude	Number of deaths
1905	Afghanistan	8.6	20,000
1908	Italy	7.5	84,000
1915	Italy	7.0	150,000
1923	Japan	8.2	142,807
1927	China	8.3	130,228
1932	China	7.6	70,000
1935	Pakistan	7.5	30,000
1939	Chile	8.3	28,000
1939	Turkey	8.0	32,700
1948	Turkmenistan	7.2	19,800
1960	Morocco	5.9	12,550
1962	Iran	73	12,225
1968	Iran	7.3	13,550
1970	Peru	7.8	66,800
1976	Guatemala	7.5	22,589
1976	China	8.0	655,237
1978	Iran	7.5	20,000
1988	Armenia	6.8	25,000
1988	Iran	7.7	50,000

Rewrite the table in order of the number of deaths, largest first. Use your table to compare the number of deaths to the size of the earthquake. Write down what you notice.

....

Which data give deaths to the nearest 10? (Write the number of deaths).

....

Which data give deaths to the nearest 100?

....

Which data give deaths to the nearest 1000?

....

Which data give deaths to the nearest 10000?

....

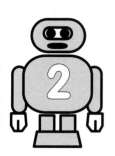

The odd calculator

This calculator is behaving oddly. If you want to put in a large number – for example 3752 – it won't let you just type it in. You have to feed each digit in separately, e.g. 3000 + 700 + 50 +2.

Write down what you would press to make the calculator show these numbers.

1 7023 ....

2 3205 ....

3 5320 ....

4 2003 ....

5 7030 ....

Reverse challenge

Use number cards to make a 4-digit number, e.g. 1436

Reverse the digits to make a new number, e.g. 6341

Write down both numbers and put one in your calculator. Add and subtract to get from one number to the other.

Write down what you do.

Repeat for other sets of 4 digits.

1436

    +5000

6436

    -100

6336

    +10

6346

    -5

6341

Place value holders

2132

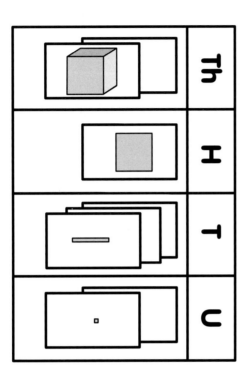

Th	H	T	U

2.314

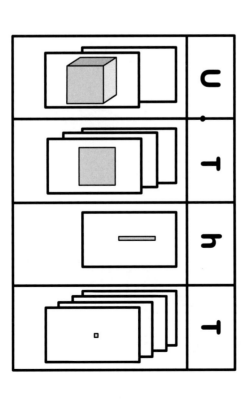

U	t	h	th

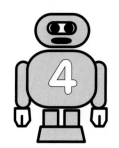

4 Max and min

Because the USA is a large country, its cities can have temperatures very different from each other. Here are the record maximum and minimum temperatures (°C) for two American cities:

Anchorage Alaska	Jan	Feb	Mar	Apr	May	Jun	Jul	Aug	Sep	Oct	Nov	Dec
Maximum temp.	10	9	11	18	25	29	28	28	23	16	12	9
Minimum temp.	-36	-32	-31	-20	-8	1	3	-1	-7	-21	-29	-34

Miami Florida	Jan	Feb	Mar	Apr	May	Jun	Jul	Aug	Sep	Oct	Nov	Dec
Maximum temp.	31	32	33	36	35	37	37	37	36	35	32	31
Minimum temp.	-1	0	0	8	12	16	21	20	20	11	4	-1

Are there any months in Miami when it has ever reached freezing? ....

Are there any months in Anchorage when it has never reached freezing? ....

In Anchorage, how much colder can it get in December than it gets in August? .... in June? ....

In Miami, how much colder can it get in December than it gets in August? .... in June? ....

Make up a question to ask your class:

....

....

My own rules

Take two cards and put them side by side.
Make up a rule which connects them, e.g.

32, 86

The rule could be : **Double and add 22**.

Use your rule to work out the next three numbers, e.g.

86	Double and add 22	→	194
194	Double and add 22	→	410
410	Double and add 22	→	842

Sequence:
32, 86, 194, 410, 842

Give your sequence to a friend. Ask them to work out your rule.

Rule ....

Sequence ....

Rule ....

Sequence ....

Rule ....

Sequence ....

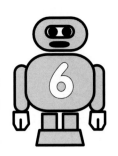

Is it true?

Below are some statements. Write below each one:
This is true because .... **or** This isn't true because ....

The sum of two odd numbers is always even.

....

The sum of three odd numbers is always odd.

....

An even number is always the sum of two odd numbers.

....

An even number is always half an even number.

....

An even number is always double an odd number.

....

An odd number is always half an even number.

....

Make up some statements of your own for others to try.

....

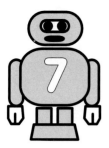

Name

Abacus multiples

You can only use three beads.

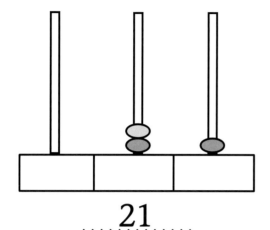

This abacus shows a multiple of 3.
Draw some other multiples of 3.

. . . . 21 . . . .

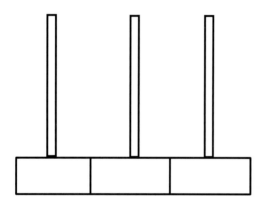

. . . .

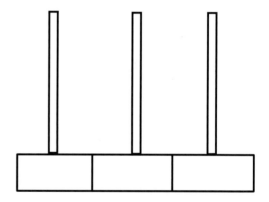

. . . .

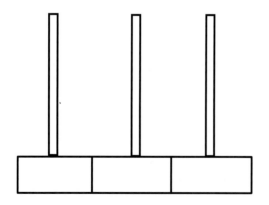

. . . .

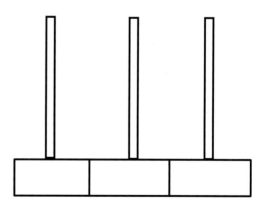

. . . .

See how many multiples of 4 you can find.
Remember, you can only use three beads and
a three-pronged abacus.
Carry on for other numbers. Draw a table of your answers.

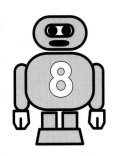

Name

Disco lights

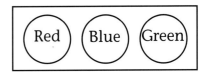

The disco lights are made up of red, blue and green flashes.
The red light flashes every 3 seconds,
the blue light flashes every 4 seconds and
the green light every 5 seconds.
Colour in when the lights are on during the first 20 seconds:

1 sec	○ ○ ○
2 secs	○ ○ ○
3 secs	○ ○ ○
4 secs	○ ○ ○
5 secs	○ ○ ○
6 secs	○ ○ ○
7 secs	○ ○ ○
8 secs	○ ○ ○
9 secs	○ ○ ○
10 secs	○ ○ ○
11 secs	○ ○ ○
12 secs	○ ○ ○
13 secs	○ ○ ○
14 secs	○ ○ ○
15 secs	○ ○ ○
16 secs	○ ○ ○
17 secs	○ ○ ○
18 secs	○ ○ ○
19 secs	○ ○ ○
20 secs	○ ○ ○

Make the following guesses:

I think the red and blue will flash together again at .... seconds.

I think the blue and green will flash together again at .... seconds.

I think the red and green will flash together again at .... seconds.

I think all three colours will flash together at .... seconds.

Carry on recording your flashes – you might want to find a different recording method.

See if your guesses were correct.

How many times in one hour will the colours all flash together?

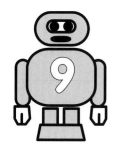

Square patterns

You need coloured linking cubes.

Make this growing pattern using a different colour for each shape.
. . .up to 10 shapes

Join the ten pieces up to make a square.

Finish this number pattern.
1
1+3=
1+3+5=
1+3+5+7=
1+3+5+7+9=
1+3+5+7+9+11=
1+3+5+7+9+11+13=
1+3+5+7+9+11+13+15=
1+3+5+7+9+11+13+15+17=
1+3+5+7+9+11+13+15+17+19=

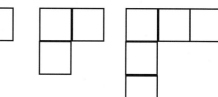

Colour these answers on a multiplication square

1	2	3	4	5	6	7	8	9	10
2	4	6	8	10	12	14	16	18	20
3	6	9	12	15	18	21	24	27	30
4	8	12	16	20	24	28	32	36	40
5	10	15	20	25	30	35	40	45	50
6	12	18	24	30	36	42	48	54	60
7	14	21	28	35	42	49	56	63	70
8	16	24	32	40	48	56	64	72	80
9	18	27	36	45	54	63	72	81	90
10	20	30	40	50	60	70	80	90	100

Write about how these tasks are connected: ....

....

....

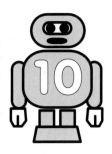

Factor pairs

You need number cards 2–30, shuffled and placed face down.
You also need a bag of counters or cubes.
Take a card and count out that number of counters.
Arrange them to make a rectangle.

The length and width of your rectangle make a factor
pair of the number of counters.

3,4 is a factor pair of 12.

1,12 is a factor pair of 12.

Record your answer in a table, and look for a different
rectangle. When you can find no more rectangles,
take a new card and begin again.

Number	Factor pairs
12	1,12 2,6 3,4

On a separate table, list all the factors of the numbers
from 2–30:

Number	Factor
2	1, 2
3	

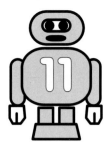

Name
....

Equivalent fractions

Look at some of the equivalent fractions you already know:

$$\frac{1}{2} = \frac{2}{4} \qquad \frac{1}{2} = \frac{5}{10}$$

You can find these fractions on the multiplication square.

1	2	3	4	5	6	7	8	9	10
2	4	6	8	10	12	14	16	18	20

Use these two lines from the square to write other equivalent fractions.

$$\frac{1}{2} =$$

___

1	2	3	4	5	6	7	8	9	10
2	4	6	8	10	12	14	16	18	20
3	6	9	12	15	18	21	24	27	30
4	8	12	16	20	24	28	32	36	40
5	10	15	20	25	30	35	40	45	50
6	12	18	24	30	36	42	48	54	60
7	14	21	28	35	42	49	56	63	70
8	16	24	32	40	48	56	64	72	80
9	18	27	36	45	54	63	72	81	90
10	20	30	40	50	60	70	80	90	100

Take any other two lines from the square, for example:

2	4	6	8	10	12	14	16	18	20
3	6	9	12	15	18	21	24	27	30

or

3	6	9	12	15	18	21	24	27	30

5	10	15	20	25	30	35	40	45	50

Write down the equivalent fractions you can make:

....

Write about why this method works:

....
....
....

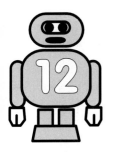

Farey lattices

We can show fractions on a line graph:

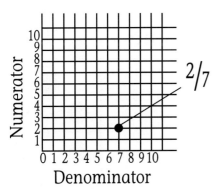

$2/7$

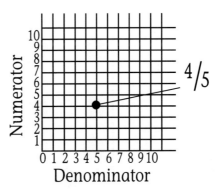

$4/5$

On a graph below, draw all the fractions which are the same as a half (e.g. $\frac{1}{2}$, $\frac{2}{4}$, $\frac{3}{6}$).

Join them together with a line. Add some other fractions (e.g. $\frac{1}{5}$, $\frac{4}{5}$).

What does their position tell you? ....

....

On another graph draw a line and read off the fractions which are on that line. Write about anything you notice.

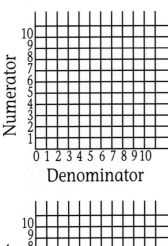

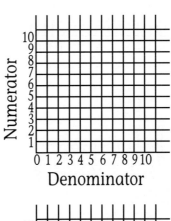

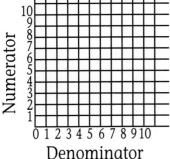

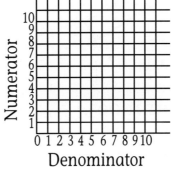

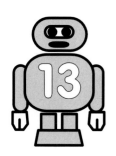

Domino fractions

You need two sets of dominoes or pictures of dominoes.

Take any domino.
Arrange it like a
fraction.
This is $^4/_5$.

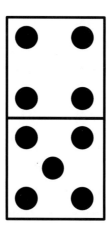

Turn the domino
around.
This is now
$^5/_4$ or $1^1/_4$.

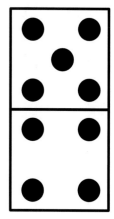

Draw your
domino here:

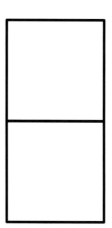

and the rotated
domino here:

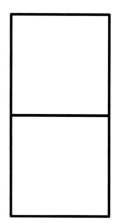

Add your fractions to this number line.

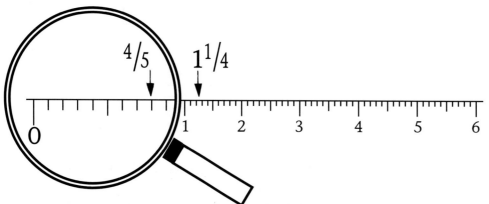

What do you notice? ....

Try for other dominoes.
Use what you have found to put all the domino
fractions in order. Use a calculator to check.

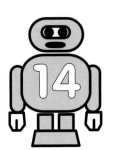

Connect 4

12	4	2	6	9	10	5	3
9	2	6	5	8	4	10	9
4	2	10	4	2	5	3	6
6	5	12	2	8	9	4	12
10	9	3	2	6	10	8	5
9	8	5	12	12	8	3	8
6	3	12	5	3	4	9	2
12	4	2	10	8	10	3	6

$1/2$ of 12	$1/3$ of 12	$1/4$ of 12	$1/6$ of 12	$1/3$ of 15
$1/5$ of 15	$1/10$ of 20	$1/10$ of 30	$1/10$ of 40	$1/10$ of 50
$1/10$ of 60	$2/3$ of 12	$3/4$ of 12	$5/6$ of 12	$2/3$ of 15
$2/5$ of 15	$3/5$ of 15	$4/5$ of 15	$1/2$ of 24	$1/3$ of 24
$1/4$ of 24	$1/6$ of 24	$1/9$ of 18	$1/3$ of 30	$1/6$ of 30
$1/4$ of 36	$1/4$ of 32	$1/3$ of 36	$1/5$ of 60	$1/6$ of 60
$1/9$ of 36	$1/8$ of 40	$1/5$ of 40	$1/2$ of 18	$1/6$ of 18

Decimal shades

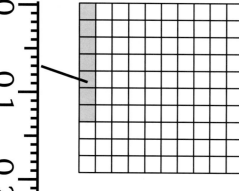

0.07 shaded

0.93 unshaded

0.11 shaded

.... unshaded

.... shaded

0.73 unshaded

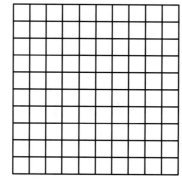

.... shaded

0.55 unshaded

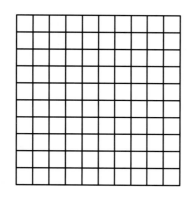

0.72 shaded

.... unshaded

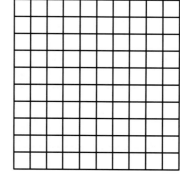

.... shaded

0.2 unshaded

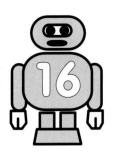

Decimal jigsaw

0.01	0.02	0.03	0.04	0.05	0.06	0.07	0.08	0.09	0.1
0.11	0.12	0.13	0.14	0.15	0.16	0.17	0.18	0.19	0.2
0.21	0.22	0.23	0.24	0.25	0.26	0.27	0.28	0.29	0.3
0.31	0.32	0.33	0.34	0.35	0.36	0.37	0.38	0.39	0.4
0.41	0.42	0.43	0.44	0.45	0.46	0.47	0.48	0.49	0.5
0.51	0.52	0.53	0.54	0.55	0.56	0.57	0.58	0.59	0.6
0.61	0.62	0.63	0.64	0.65	0.66	0.67	0.68	0.69	0.7
0.71	0.72	0.73	0.74	0.75	0.76	0.77	0.78	0.79	0.8
0.81	0.82	0.83	0.84	0.85	0.86	0.87	0.88	0.89	0.9
0.91	0.92	0.93	0.94	0.95	0.96	0.97	0.98	0.99	1

Cut out the square and cut along the dark lines
to make a jigsaw.
Put the jigsaw back together again!

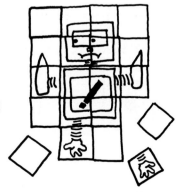

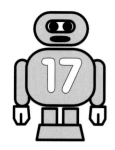

Target

TARGET

0.

This is a game. Any number can play.
Take turns to be the target setter.

You need 0–9 dice, spinners or cards.
The target setter uses these to fill in the target number.

Each player should write their name on a play card.
Take turns to throw the dice once and write the number
in one of the boxes.
Repeat so that everyone has their play card completed.
Together, put the cards in order.
If you are touching the target card you get two points,
one card away (on either side) gets you one point.
Continue until someone has 10 points.

Name . . . .

0.

Name . . . .

0.

Name . . . .

0.

Name . . . .

0.

Name . . . .

0.

Name . . . .

0.

Name . . . .

0.

Name . . . .

0.

Name . . . .

0.

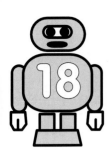

Percentage shades

Shade in pictures on the 4 hundred grids below.

e.g.

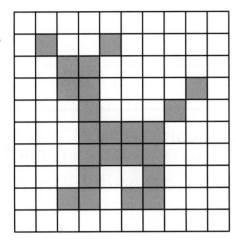

23% shaded

Cut out the pictures and stick them on the greater than strip so that the positions are correct.

Write the percentages under each one.

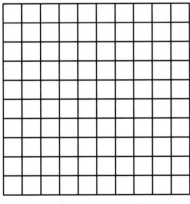

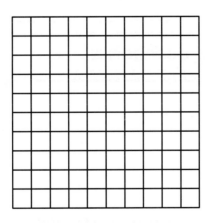

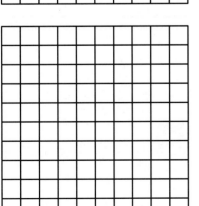

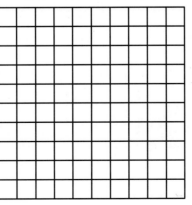

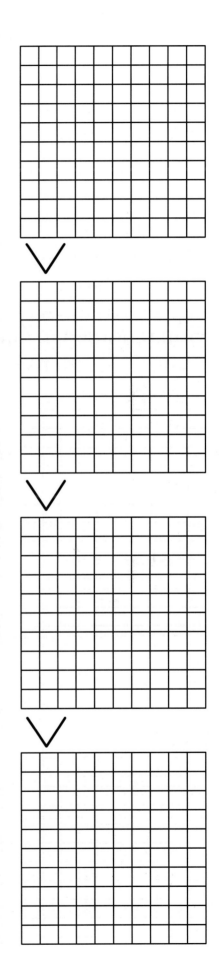

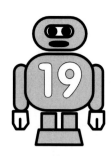

Garden planner

My garden is			
Flower bed	20%	0.2	20/100
Pond	20%	0.2	20/100
Vegetables	21%	0.21	21/100
Lawn	39%	0.39	39/100

Plan a garden, a bedroom and something of your own choice. Write the sections in percentages, in decimals and in fractions.

My garden is

My bedroom is

My

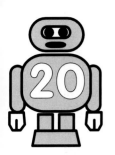

Money dominoes

50p	£1.00	10p	£0.50	1p	£0.20
£1	£0.10	5p	£0.02	2p	£0.05
20p	£0.01	50p	20%	10p	1%
1p	2%	£1	5%	5p	100%
2p	50%	20p	10%	£0.20	2%
£0.10	100%	£0.02	10%	£0.50	1%
£1.00	20%	£0.05	50%	£0.01	5%

Cut out the pieces and play dominoes.
You can't match a coin to a coin, a percentage to a percentage
or a decimal to a decimal.

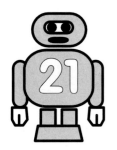

Work it out!

You need dice or cards labelled with: $+$, $-$, $\times$, $\div$.
You also need number cards 1–50, and a partner.

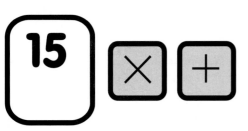

Shuffle the cards and place face down. Take one, but don't let your partner see. Roll the two dice and place side by side.
Make up a sum using your own numbers, e.g.

I times by 3, I add 5 and I get 50. What was my number?

Your partner now has to work it out.

Take turns to be the 'setter' and the 'worker out'.

Think of a number

I think of a number.
I times it by 3, I add 5 and I get 50.
What was my number?

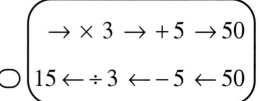

$$\rightarrow \times 3 \rightarrow +5 \rightarrow 50$$
$$15 \leftarrow \div 3 \leftarrow -5 \leftarrow 50$$

15
The answer is 15!

Set each other some puzzles like this.

Name

Arranging digits

Use the number cards: | 1 | 2 | 3 | 4 | 5 | 6 | 7 | 8 | 9 |

Arrange the cards so that the sums are correct:

```
    ☐ ☐ ☐          ☐ ☐ ☐
  + ☐ ☐ ☐        − ☐ ☐ ☐
  ─────────      ─────────
    ☐ ☐ ☐          ☐ ☐ ☐
```

Make the largest sum.

```
  ☐ ☐ ☐ ☐
  + ☐ ☐ ☐
      ☐ ☐
  ─────────
```

Make the largest difference.

```
  ☐ ☐ ☐ ☐ ☐
  − ☐ ☐ ☐ ☐
  ───────────
```

Make the smallest sum.

```
  ☐ ☐ ☐ ☐
  + ☐ ☐ ☐
      ☐ ☐
  ─────────
```

Make the smallest difference.

```
  ☐ ☐ ☐ ☐ ☐
  − ☐ ☐ ☐ ☐
  ───────────
```

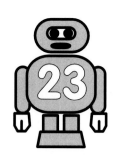

Brackets

Take a calculation string:

$2 + 3 \times 4 - 5 \times 6$

If we do this in the order we read it, and not using a calculator, we get 90 (check!).

Some calculators work like this, but others don't.
Try it with your calculator. Do you get -16?
If so, your calculator is taking $\times$ and $\div$ to be more important than $+$ and $-$.

We can write what it is doing by using brackets.

$2 + (3 \times 4) - (5 \times 6)$

You **must** do the brackets first: $2 + 12 - 30 = -16$

Experiment with brackets.
Choose what operations to write between the numbers, then choose where to put the brackets.
Guess an answer first, then work it out on your calculator.

	Guess	Calculator check
1 2 3 =		
1 2 3 =		
3 4 2 5 =		
3 4 2 5 =		
3 4 2 5 =		
10 100 5 10 =		
10 100 5 10 =		
10 100 5 10 =		

Seven sentence strings

Cut apart these cards.

Use them to make seven number sentence strings, e.g.

$14 \times 50 = 14 \times 100 \div 2 = 1400 \div 2 = 700$

19 × 7	20 × 7	140	=	−
1 × 7	−	=	133	7
21 × 7	+	=	147	Double
77	Double	70	+	Double
14	154	×	5	×
10	700	14	15	×
×	2	30	7	=
210	50	100	÷	700
÷	2	210	16	8
56	112	3	÷	+
5	÷	42	7 × 7	7
490	49	500	39	539
11	10 × 77	1 × 77	770	77
800	47	105	847	1400

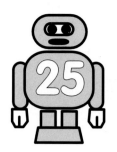

Grid gaps

Here is one way to do a calculation like 243×7:

	200	40	3
7	1400	280	21

```
    1400
     280
      21
    ----
    1701
```

Fill in the gaps in these calculations:

	70	3
6	600		

600
____

	500		
3		150	21

150
 21
___

	700	10	9
	2800		

2800
____

____

Here is one way to do a calculation like 24×37:

	20	4
30	600	120
7	140	28

```
     600
     120
     140
      28
    ----
     888
```

Fill in the missing gaps in these calculations:

		5
40		
	60	10

60
10
___

		4
	2800	
	120	

2800
120
____